EARTH SPIRITUALITY:
IN THE CATHOLIC AND
DOMINICAN TRADITIONS

SOR JUANA PRESS

Sor Juana Press is a project of Santuario Sisterfarm, a nonprofit organization rooted in the Texas Hill Country and grounded in the rich multicultural legacy of the Borderlands. Founded in 2002, Santuario Sisterfarm inspirits the work of transforming human relationships with Earth and other humans by moving from dominance to co-creative partnerships, drawing on insights from wisdom traditions, nature, the new science, and women's ways. Santuario Sisterfarm advances its mission by cultivating diversity – biodiversity and cultural diversity.

Sor Juana Press is dedicated to publishing the works of women – particularly women of color and women religious – on topics rooted in women's spirituality and relationship with Earth, *la Tierra, nuestra madre*.

The Press invokes the name and honors the memory of Sor Juana Inés de la Cruz (1648-1695), a Mexican nun, scholar, poet, playwright, musician, and scientist – a woman with a *sed de conocer* (a thirst for knowing) – who was silenced for advocating women's education. Hers is the first voice in the Americas to speak out in favor of a woman's right to learn and to express concern about human depredation of the environment.

EARTH SPIRITUALITY:
IN THE CATHOLIC AND DOMINICAN TRADITIONS

Sharon Therese Zayac, O.P.

CONVERSATIO
Dominican Women on Earth

Issue No.1   June 2003

SOR JUANA PRESS

Edited by Elise D. García and Carol Coston, OP

Cover illustration in batik created by Joy Troyer for THE EVERYTHING SEED: A STORY OF BEGINNINGS – a children's picture book about the creation of the Universe, published by Beaver's Pond Press.

We gratefully acknowledge the financial support of the Adrian Dominican Sisters in the publication of this first issue of the Dominican Women on Earth series.

Cover and book design by Susan E. Klein of Sister Creek Studios, San Antonio, Texas. (www.sistercreekstudios.com)

Printed by Crumrine Printers, Inc., San Antonio, Texas

This book is printed with soy inks on 100% post-consumer recycled paper, processed chlorine-free, supplied by Dolphin Blue, a Dallas, Texas-based company specializing in environmentally responsible office products. (www.dolphinblue.com)

ISBN 0-9740243-0-9
ISSN 1543-978X

TABLE OF CONTENTS

ABOUT THE AUTHOR

Sharon Therese Zayac, O.P., a Springfield (Illinois) Dominican Sister, is the Director of Benincasa Ministries, which includes Jubilee Farm, her congregation's 111-acre center for ecology and spirituality in central Illinois. A Reiki practitioner and a student of Healing Touch, Sharon holds a degree in secondary education from St. Ambrose University in Davenport, Iowa; a master's degree in Hospital Administration from Xavier University in Cincinnati, Ohio; and a master's in Earth Literacy from Saint Mary-of-the-Woods College in Indiana (having the distinction of being the first graduate from the College's Earth Literacy program). Sharon has served on numerous boards, task forces, and committees. During the 1990s, she served as president and chief executive officer of St. Mary-Rogers Memorial Hospital in Rogers, Arkansas. She was recognized as one of Arkansas' "Business Women in Leadership" in 1993 and as one of "Top 100 Women in Arkansas" in 1995. In 2001, Sharon was one of ten women showcased by Lifetime Television in a photo gallery on the network's website, recognizing women who are making a difference in their communities – in Sharon's case, for her work on ecological issues. A growing number of speaking engagements keeps Sharon on the road, away from Jubilee Farm where she otherwise finds herself "happily mucking about with the llamas and chickens, planting and weeding and harvesting the garden."

SHARING THE JOURNEY

I must admit that I rarely read the preface to anything. I think it ironic that I have been asked to write one myself. And as difficult as I found it to write, I also admit it has helped me articulate for myself the journey I am on. For those of you, unlike me, who will read this preface, I hope it will give you some insights into your own journey.

It has been only recently that I have been able to look back over the circumstances of my life and see within them the pattern, the weaving that has led me to my current (and still so tender) understanding of my place in this universe.

I was the daughter of a career Air Force master sergeant and spent much of my growing-up years traveling the world. My earliest childhood memories so impressed the smell of ocean breezes within me, that I have never felt quite at home anywhere else. Four years on the island of Oahu made me one with the sound of the waves and the deep blue of the Pacific. Those four years were followed by another four in the incredible countryside of southwestern Germany. We frequently traveled throughout Europe and made several memorable trips over the Alps. A brief stint in North Dakota (quite a shock to all of us) saw us gladly waving goodbye to the intense cold plains and once again settling in on another Pacific island. We were to spend five years on Okinawa, and my adolescence flowered amidst the mix of Okinawan, Japanese, Chinese, and American cultures. Most unwillingly, we left Okinawa and spent the next two years in the panhandle of Florida (close to the beach!). My father then retired from the Air Force and we moved to southern California. It was from there, after two years in Redlands, that I entered the Springfield (Illinois) Dominicans.

My mother kept asking me, "Why Illinois?" I couldn't say, other than those were the sisters who answered the phone when I called. I didn't know there were California Dominicans. Had I known, my life certainly would have taken different turns. I am hopeful it still would have led me to the same place. But the Spirit works as she will, and instead of remaining close to my beloved Pacific, nestled in the coastal mountains, it was my destiny to come and live on the vast, flat, humid plains of central Illinois.

God has an incredible sense of humor. Other than the two years we spent in North Dakota, my entire life had been spent within the sight of forests, mountains, or ocean. I honestly didn't know what to make of this place to which I had come. And though I came over thirty years ago, I still miss the smell of salt air and the comforting embrace of mountainsides. I am still disoriented by the vast flatness that extends all the way to the horizon. And though I quite fearlessly lived through countless typhoons, the threat of tidal waves, and several earthquakes, I find myself unnerved when the wind begins its howl and flattens the neighboring cornfields and every small bush and tree in our yard.

Yes, God does have a sense of humor. And though I have not yet been able to laugh with her, I am learning finally to call this place home. It does not feed my soul as do the ocean and forests, but I find my roots sinking into the soil of the 111 acres we call Jubilee Farm. So much so, that I have come to begrudge the time I am away from it. How did I ever come to the point in my life where I could be content with where I am and with who I am becoming? It has been an amazing journey.

I entered our congregation in 1971 at a time when all good Dominicans taught in schools. I spent my first ten years in ministry teaching junior and senior high in four of our schools. And though I loved teaching (and still do), I found the classroom environment stifling. I was given the opportunity to enter the field of healthcare administration, and after several years of study and internship, I arrived in our hospital in northwest Arkansas in 1987. Little did I know at the time what that would mean in my life.

Certainly not by chance but in the broad design of the universe, one of the sisters with whom I lived introduced me to the writings of Matthew Fox and Meister Eckhart. It was all I needed. And though the transformation was slow, it had begun its work within me. I have never been the same.

The last six years I spent in Arkansas were as president/chief executive officer of our hospital. It was the beginning of the great turmoil that still grips healthcare. Pressuring hospitals to become more business-like, state and federal governments had introduced a method of payment they felt would ensure that transition. What developed is the current atmosphere of fierce competition, unsavory corporate practices, and the struggle to keep healthcare a ministry rather than big business. I was not up to that struggle. I found myself having to make too many compromises. I found that what I was being asked to live was not what was growing within my consciousness. When I had the opportunity to leave the hospital, I took it. I went on a sabbatical.

Who ever would have guessed that on the eastern end of Long Island I would find the passion that has since held me in its grip? In March of 1996 I left Arkansas to spend several months with the Amityville Dominicans at Siena Spirituality Center in Water Mill, New York. The most unlikely set of circumstances (only seen in Hollywood ... or in the universe) launched me, literally, on my present path. I was corresponding with the center's director about my upcoming fall sabbatical when she placed a flyer about their spring sabbatical in one of the mailings.

I was leaving the hospital in March and had hoped to find a spring sabbatical somewhere to give me some much needed space and rest. All spring sabbaticals seemed to begin in January and end in late May. I needed one to start in March and end in early May. This one did. And its title struck a deep chord ... *Come Home to the Whole*. Long story short, I was accepted. Longer story short, this was the first time they had offered a spring sabbatical, I was the only one in the program, and after serious consideration on their part, it would be the last spring sabbatical they would offer.

I was alone for two months with Jeanne Clarke, O.P., the center's director, who did some fast regrouping with the outside presenters she had lined up. The presenters offered their programs on the weekends, and Jeanne and I spent the week days listening to Miriam Therese MacGillis', O.P., tapes, watching Brian Swimme's *Canticle to the Cosmos*, and exploring the beautiful nature preserves on the island. I had hours to myself to begin devouring the books Jeanne was collecting for a small resource library. Through their works, I met Thomas Berry,

Sallie McFague, Sean McDonagh, Michael Dowd, Chellis Glendinning, John Seed and others.

I was on fire. Absolutely so excited I could barely contain myself. Everything made so much sense! Why hadn't anyone told me about this before? Why doesn't everyone know about this? And now that I am learning about it, what can I do with it? I knew my life had profoundly and unalterably changed, but I had no clue what it would mean for me personally or ministerially. I just knew that it would be integral to whatever work I next took up. I could be patient with whatever that might be, but would my congregation's leadership? And how would I even begin to explain to them what this was all about? I couldn't even articulate it myself.

I am not sure exactly when some kind of ministry plan began to make itself known to me. I do know that my first trip to Genesis Farm in northwestern New Jersey awakened a deep desire to plant myself somewhere on a piece of land and begin to experience it in intimate detail. I will not go into the details of the next few years, though it is nothing short of miraculous. Well, perhaps miraculous is overstated. It is most certainly the result of the universe conspiring to put into motion something it has long awaited.

In May of 1999 our congregation purchased 109 acres on the west side of Springfield, Illinois. In honor of the Jubilee Year, we named it Jubilee Farm.

Since then we have picked up an additional couple of acres. Unabashedly, we model ourselves after Genesis Farm (Caldwell Dominicans), Crown Point (Akron Dominicans), Shepherd's Corner (Columbus Dominicans), Crystal Spring (Kentucky Dominicans), The Bridge Between (Sinsinawa Dominicans), Michaela Farm (Oldenburg Franciscans), and a host of other centers established by women religious who have taken up the challenge to live and model sustainability in a culture so unaware of its destructive lifestyle. So many things about Jubilee Farm have just fallen into place. I can have no doubt that the work is far bigger than I am, and that it is not my work. It will continue whether I am here or not.

In our grand enthusiasm to do everything at once, yet not really understanding what needs to be done – as we question what we should do and how we should do it – the land quietly sits and waits for us to learn from her. We feel such an urgency to

South pasture of Jubilee Farm

make right all the wrongs we have done to her, and she patiently teaches us to slow down and look and listen. I am finally beginning to do so. I am finally allowing myself to become rooted in the gentle slopes and quiet pastures. For the first time ever, I have taken winter seriously and rested from the frenetic activity of summer and fall. I have risked offending that vague inner disquiet that I should be busy about something worthwhile.

And as my roots work their way into this land, I have discovered that all my head knowledge (which I have always been very good about collecting) has begun to penetrate my heart and my consciousness. All the books and videos I've consumed have given me the words to articulate the passion and energy of the universe within me. But it is the connection to this land that gives me a concrete expression of that passion.

All the most beautifully profound words ever written are not enough to ground us in the passion. Perhaps that is why we use the word "ground." We must have connection to the land, to Earth, for the journey to make sense, to be valid, to be real.

I am not sure when I came to this realization, as I am not sure when my views changed about a good many things I once held sacred. I find myself either questioning much of what I once believed or dismissing it as one would dismiss something we believed as children but no longer as adults. It is not that I don't believe anything I was ever taught. It is that I now look at almost everything in the light of what I now believe. It doesn't negate past knowledge or belief. It puts it into the proper context. Or in some cases, allows it to fall out of the context!

We are all in the one cosmic journey. We are part of the same unfolding story. We are all interrelated and interdependent. There is no such thing as independence or autonomy on any level in the universe. The context of our humanity is the planet Earth. There is no other context. And all that we do and all that we are, we live and do as a part of the entire community that makes up Earth. Nothing we humans do in any one part of Earth is contained there. It affects the entire Earth.

Living out of that knowledge has impacted my entire life. On the one hand, it has given me a profound sense of connection. On the other, it has made me difficult to live with, sometimes even for myself. I am generally not a detail person. But I have come to see that life is lived in the details. I can't preach against industries' pouring toxins into the air and water unless I refuse to pour even the smallest amount down the bathroom drain. I can't bewail the landslide of plastic, which is literally burying us, without trying to keep every piece I can out of the landfill. I can't be aware of the poisoning of our food supply and the horrendous treatment of the animals, who become our food, without making serious choices about what I consume. And the more I learn, the harder it is to know how to live and what choices to make. But that doesn't take me off the hook of learning.

My friends might say otherwise, but the most profound change in my life has not been my lifestyle, though I moved from the corporate office of a CEO to happily mucking about with the llamas and chickens, planting and weeding and harvesting the garden, learning to live companionably with the six- and eight-leggeds, finding less and less of that which I want to buy and more and more of that which I want to let go.

My most profound challenge has been to let go of my image of God. I had thought I had done that when I embraced creation spirituality. Understanding God through the context of the universe story continues to stretch me further ... stretch, but not frighten. I am learning not to put all my knowledge into neat little boxes. It happens so insidiously! And once I became conscious of doing it, God escaped from my "God box." I began to see that the God I thought I knew didn't exist at all. God was bigger and far more surprising. And God has not stopped growing since! Each new awakening allows God to grow. Each time I discover another bias I have, another skewed idea about persons or peoples or other parts of creation, God grows. These have become my most amazing discoveries! And it is these insights that continue to feed me, giving me hope in what may well be hopeless times, giving me courage to speak when many deny the signs all around them, and granting me the faith that the journey will continue, not only in spite of us but because of us.

EARTH SPIRITUALITY:
IN THE CATHOLIC AND DOMINICAN TRADITIONS

Many Christians struggle with an Earth-centered spirituality (ecospirituality), a spirituality that places humans within the context of creation and not at its apex. As a modern culture, we have lost the understanding of our relationship to the rest of creation, an understanding that was common to all just a few short centuries ago.

Earth is our home. It is the stuff of which we are made, and it is the larger body that will welcome us back when we die, only to resurrect us again. We belong here, as we belong to God. Earth is an expression of the God for whom we long. Until we recognize Earth as the home that nurtures and nourishes us, we will continue to despoil, devour, foul, and desecrate her with no realization that we are doing the same to ourselves.

Reclaiming our image of an immanent God bound up with everything on this planet must become our metaphor, if life is to survive. Our Catholic Christian faith provides a rich heritage of Earth-spirituality for us to draw upon in making this shift.

Catholic women religious have a leadership role to play in teaching and modeling a responsible and sustainable relationship with Earth. A sustainable lifestyle for all Earth's inhabitants is the praxis, the practical outcome, of living as though we believe Earth is the body of God. By virtue of their founding and history, there is a particular imperative for Dominican women to take up this role.

INTRODUCTION

I write as a Catholic and a Dominican Sister to other Dominicans and women religious. However, the truths about which I write hold for all of us, and most people reading these reflections will hear echoes of their own history, since the teachings of the Catholic Church and of Dominicans like Albert the Great and Thomas Aquinas have influenced all of Western culture. Each of us is challenged to look back at the founding principles of our respective cultures and faiths in light of emerging scientific and ecological awarenesses.

In this essay, I begin by looking at recent Catholic Church teaching on the environment, briefly reviewing Vatican documents and the pastoral letters from a number of the world's bishops. I then look at both themes in our Judeo/Christian tradition that cause us to disregard nature and rationales that support a respect for Earth – and analyze these con-flicting propensities, *i.e.*, our dual heritage from the ancient Hebrews and the Greeks.

In the last section, I share the history of the founding of the Dominican Order and the teachings of several prominent early Dominicans: Albert the Great, Thomas Aquinas, Meister Eckhart. And based upon the reason our Order was founded and the four pillars of Dominican life (study, preaching, common life, and prayer), I conclude that we Dominicans have a mandate, an obligation, to be engaged in Earth ministry.

REVERENCING EARTH:
WHY DOES IT MAKE US SQUIRM?

It is safe to say that many, if not most, of us Catholics in the Western world struggle with reconciling what we are beginning to learn about the origins of life with both what we have grown up believing about nature and what we think our Church teaches us about creation. We are wary, if not frightened, of dabbling with pantheism and nature worship.

A good analogy is to liken the fear of our growing understanding about creation and our role within it to many non-Catholics' assumption that we worship Mary or the saints. We don't worship her or the saints, nor is this growing awakening to Earth a misplaced worship of nature.

But what is this new talk about "reverencing" Earth all about? Why is it that some people insist on capitalizing the "e" in Earth? Do some of us squirm at this because we see it as a divinizing of Earth, of equating our planet with God?

Actually, the question should be, "Why don't we capitalize it?" Earth is a proper noun! We capitalize

Mercury, Venus, Mars, and the other planets in our solar system. Do we think less of the planet we call home? Perhaps the old axiom, "familiarity breeds contempt," holds true.

But the question persists: How *does* all this "fit" with Catholicism, let alone Dominican spirituality, for those among us who are Dominican? What *do* we, as Catholics, believe about creation?

Perhaps a better question is: What does our Catholic heritage – and our Dominican heritage – *teach* us about creation?

The answer will take us on a journey from recent Catholic Church teachings on the environment, much further back in history. Knowing our history will put our present and growing understanding of creation in the proper context. It should help us see that our emerging understanding is not a new cult and that we ought not to fall into the trap of dismissing it as some kind of "New Age" stuff. The creation story we are newly awakening to is, in fact, a vital part of our Christian heritage.

BIRTH OF THE MODERN ENVIRONMENTAL MOVEMENT IN CHURCH AND SOCIETY

Many experts say that the modern environmental movement began with the publication of Rachel Carson's book, SILENT SPRING, in 1962. Although there were many notable environmentalists before her, this book created a stir in the American public and among some notable scientists who agreed with her conclusions that we were poisoning Earth and ourselves to death. The modern environmental movement was launched despite the best efforts of other scientists, industrialists, and many politicians to discredit Carson.

The tenor of the early 1960s carried forward the optimism of the 1950s. The unrest, rebellion, and rejection of the establishment were still several years off. The world was generally enamored of modern science and all the marvels and promises held by technology. In modernity, the world had great hopes, even expectations, that science would cure the evils that had long plagued humankind.

The Church was no different. It had entered Vatican II, and the tone of the documents produced by the Council echoed the beliefs of the rest of the world.[1] They generally praised the accomplishments of modern technology and did not pick up on the writings of Rachel Carson or on the growing concern about the havoc that technology was creating on Earth.

That concern, however, manifested itself in the inauguration of Earth Day in 1970. A year later, a group of European industrialists gathered to analyze the impact of industrial growth on the environment. That same year, 1971, the Church, echoing what it was now hearing in society, responded by naming *environmental degradation* for the first time in her official teachings, if only briefly!

Prior Church documents had spoken of the environment, but not as an issue in itself and only in terms of social justice. *Rerum Novarum* (1891) claimed that the goods of the Earth are for all to share. *Quadragesimo Anno* (1931) suggested limits on private ownership. *Pacem in Terris* (1963) stated that sharing was essential for peace and justice. And *Gaudium et Spes* (1965) reaffirmed humanity's responsibility to care for Earth.[2]

In *Octogesima Adveniens* (1971), the Church took the reference to the environment one small step further. Pope Paul VI briefly noted that, "[humankind] is suddenly becoming aware that by an ill-considered exploitation of nature, [humanity] risks destroying it and becoming in turn a victim of this degradation." He does not name any specific environmental issue, but by using the word "degradation," the Pope recognizes that it is occurring. He also states, however, that he does not see the destruction of species or of ecosystems as a moral or religious problem in itself.[3]

In that same year, 1971, the international synod of bishops issues *Justice in the* World. Thomas Landy, associate director of the Leadership Education Project at Harvard University, notes that it is the first significant magisterial declaration about the environment, essentially characterizing environmental degradation as a violence carried out by wealthy consumers against the poor.[4] Irish Columban missionary Sean McDonagh credits this document with helping many Christians understand that the poverty that afflicts most of the world's population is "directly related to the misuse and squandering of natural and human resources in First-World – mostly traditionally Christian – countries."[5]

McDonagh further notes that Earth cannot support the consumptive lifestyle of the "First World," saying it is a lifestyle that virtually enslaves the poor of the world.

Justice in the World puts the environmental issue squarely on the table, although, at this point, the Church document reflects an anthropocentric view. That is, the concern about the environment is because of its ill effects on humanity, not because creation is valued in itself.

The environment is not formally addressed again in magisterial teaching until 1979 when Pope John Paul II delivers his first encyclical, *Redemptor Hominis*. In this encyclical, the Pope warns against needless exploitation of Earth, observing that Earth's resources are being depleted at an ever-increasing rate and putting intolerable pressure on the environment.[6]

John Paul, like all others up to that time, does not see the environment, God's creation, as an integrated totality with a role for humans within it.

Instead, he simply reaffirms that creation is ordered and that its purpose is to meet human needs. But he does take a significant step in formally addressing the environment as an issue in itself and one can use the document to trace the development of John Paul's thinking about Earth and humanity's role in it.

In *Sollicitudo Rei Socialis* (1987), we see the Pope's understanding deepen. John Paul addresses ecology in a substantive manner. He now speaks of respect for the natural world and of the mutual connection among all created things in the cosmos.[7] He notes the limits of nature's resources and the need for humans to respect the integrity of the cycles of nature, taking them into account when planning development. Human issues, population issues are to be addressed in the context of the environment.[8]

Theologian Christine Firer Hinze calls *Sollicitudo* a key document. "Not only does the pope for the first time advert to ecological issues in a major encyclical … but he also offers rich reflections on the connections between environmental degradation and the misuses of technology…."[9]

THE ECOLOGICAL CRISIS:
A MAJOR BREAKTHROUGH IN CATHOLIC TEACHING

Then in 1990 in his World Day of Peace message, John Paul delivers *The Ecological Crisis: A Common Responsibility – Peace with God the Creator,*

Peace with all Creation. Professor of Christian Ethics, Marvin L. Krier Mich calls this a major breakthrough in Roman Catholic official teaching on environment, a document entirely devoted to environmental concerns. It represents not only a major shift in magisterial teaching, but also a shift in the Pope's own teaching.

No longer abstract, *The Ecological Crisis* critiques the indiscriminate application of modern science and technology, and it addresses specific environmental problems: the greenhouse effect, acid rain, soil erosion, deforestation, use of herbicides, etc. John Paul warns that consumerism and instant self-gratification are the root causes of the ecological predicament[10] and that no solution will be found unless modern society takes a serious look at its lifestyle.[11] He encourages that appropriate action be taken:

> Faced with the widespread destruction of the environment, people everywhere are coming to understand that we cannot continue to use the goods of the [E]arth as we have in the past.... Moreover, a new *ecological awareness* is beginning to emerge which, rather than being downplayed, ought to be encouraged to develop into concrete programmes and initiatives.[12]

In section II of the document, John Paul grants moral standing to the ecological crisis, and in section IV, he cites an imperative for education in ecological responsibility.

> As I have already stated, the seriousness of the ecological issue lays bare the depth of man's [sic] moral crisis.... An education in ecological responsibility is urgent: responsibility for oneself, for others, and for the [E]arth. This education cannot be rooted in mere sentiment or empty wishes. Its purpose cannot be ideological or political. It must not be based on a rejection of the modern world or a vague desire to return to some "paradise lost." Instead, a true education in responsibility entails a genuine conversion in ways of thought and behaviour. Churches and religious bodies, non-governmental and governmental organizations, indeed all members of society, have a precise role to play in such education. The first educator, however, is the family, where the child learns to respect his [sic] neighbor and to love nature.[13]

John Paul lets no one off the hook. The ecological crisis is a common responsibility.

Today the ecological crisis has assumed such proportions as to be the responsibility of everyone. As I have pointed out, its various aspects demonstrate the need for concerted efforts aimed at establishing the duties and obligations that belong to individuals, peoples, States, and the international community.... When the ecological crisis is set within the broader context of the search for peace within society, we can understand better the importance of giving attention to what the [E]arth and its atmosphere is telling us: namely, that there is an order in the universe which must be respected, and that the human person, endowed with the capability of choosing freely, has a grave responsibility to preserve this order for the well-being of future generations. *I wish to repeat that the ecological crisis is a moral issue* (emphasis added).[14]

John Paul ends his message by calling specifically upon his brothers and sisters in the Catholic Church "in order to remind them of their serious obligation to care for all creation."[15] He reminds us that he named Francis of Assisi the Patron of those who promote ecology because "he offers Christians an example of genuine and deep respect for the integrity of creation."[16]

Mich calls this document a new chapter in the Church's teaching on the moral and religious nature of respect for creation.[17] It is indeed just that. But perhaps the document's most significant contribution is its broadening of the pro-life agenda of the Church: "Respect for life and the dignity of the human person extends also to the rest of creation, which is called to join man [*sic*] in praising God."[18] (We still await the day, however, when he will officially name women, as well.)

The Ecological Crisis is a wonderful document, an extraordinary magisterial work. It should have laid the groundwork for an explosion of theological study, discussion, and writing. But, it didn't!

John Paul's next encyclical (*Centesimus Annus*, 1991) has little to say on the environment, concentrating more on the evils of consumerism. His *Evangelium Vitae* (1995) reaffirms the value of human life, but says very little about the rest of creation, once again establishing the "lordship" of "man" over Earth, once again reaffirming an anthropocentric view. What happened?

One assessment, offered by Mich, is that John Paul's covey of advisors encouraged him to back off. One of his most respected advisors, Cardinal Joseph Ratzinger, is a known critic of environmentalists and could well have influenced him to soften his tone.[19]

In the last two years, however, John Paul has again spoken out against the evils of ecological devastation. In *God Made Man the Steward of Creation* (2001), John Paul reaffirmed the urgent need for ecological conversion: "We must therefore encourage and support the ecological conversion which in recent decades has made humanity more sensitive to the catastrophe to which it is heading. Man [*sic*] is no longer the Creator's steward, but an autonomous despot who is finally beginning to understand that he must stop at the edge of the abyss."

And in 2002, John Paul issued with Patriarch Bartholomew I of Constantinople a joint declaration on the environment entitled, *We Are Still Betraying the Mandate God Has Given Us*.

WORLD'S BISHOPS PICK UP ECOLOGICAL BANNER

Beginning in the mid-seventies, the world's bishops picked up the ecological banner, carrying it forward to this day. In the United States alone, some twenty documents have been written on issues ranging from the plight of farmers to global warming.

In 1975, the bishops of Appalachia in the United States issue a powerful statement about the environment in *This Land Is Home to Me: A Pastoral Letter on Powerlessness in Appalachia*, observing:

> The way of life, which these corporate giants create, is called by some "technological rationalization." Its forces ... become

perverted, hostile to the dignity of the [E]arth and of its people. Its destructive growth patterns pollute the air, foul the water, rape the land.[20]

....

If our present system keeps on growing and growing, it will burn up us and our world. The present pattern of energy use, a great deal of which goes for military production or else the production of discardable junk, is barbaric.[21]

Five years later, the U.S. bishops of the Midwest write *Strangers and Guests: Toward Community in the Heartland*, stating:

We are concerned about the people and land in our region. The opportunity people have to live a productive and rewarding life is determined to a great extent by the way in which they or outside interests relate to the land. We wish this relationship to be one of cooperative harmony, for the land – complemented in nature by water and air – is our most important and limited natural resource.[22]

Bishops in other parts of the world also started to give voice to ecological concerns from their perspectives. [23] In 1987, the bishops of the Dominican Republic in *Pastoral Letter on the Relationship of Human Beings to Nature*, warn:

> We can no longer fail to concern ourselves with the preservation and betterment of the environment in which we live. ... The sin of humanity against nature has its repercussions against humanity itself. (Par. 1)
>
> ....
>
> Christ to whom all things are subject and have been freed from the slavery of corruption (Rom 8:21), taught us during his earthly life to admire nature and to respect it; to use it well without spoiling or harming it; to be inspired by it and to love it. (Par. 53)

The following year, the bishops of the Philippines write *What Is Happening to Our Beauti-ful Land?* (1988), noting:

> As we reflect on what is happening in the light of the Gospel we are convinced that this assault on creation is sinful and contrary to the teachings of our faith.... The men and women who attempt to live harmoniously with nature and those who study ecology have tried to alert people to

the magnitude of the destruction taking place in our time. The latter are in a good position to tell us what is happening since they study the web of dynamic relationships which supports and sustains all life within the earthly household. (Par. 3, 4)

....

More and more we must recognize that the commitment to work for justice and to preserve the integrity of creation are two inseparable dimensions of our Christian vocation to work for the coming of the kingdom of God in our times. (Par. 26)

....

... [I]t is crucial that people motivated by religious faith...take steps to defend the Earth. It is a matter of life and death.
(Par. 5)

That same year, 1988, the bishops of Northern Italy in *Ecology: The Bishops of Lombardy Address the Community*, assert:

[The environmental issue] has once and for all entered the centers of theological research and absolutely can not be separated any longer from pastoral practice.
(Par. 2)

....

... [W]e believe it is opportune to make a statement in order to aid and sustain the conscience of Christians in a dutiful effort of discernment. This will also submit the grave problem of the environment's decline to critical evaluation in light of the Christian vision... (Par. 5)

In 1990, the bishops of Australia issue *Christians and Their Duty Toward Nature*, observing:

Today it is surely a sign of the times that many people are calling for a more enlightened care for the [E]arth and for all living things. (Par. 7)

....

Our purpose in this statement is simply this: To invite all Christians, Catholics in particular, to reflect on the truth that their responsibility within creation and their duty towards nature and the Creator are an essential part of their faith. (Par. 16)

In the 100 years since *Rerum Novarum's* brief reference to sharing the goods of Earth, Church documents have gone deeper and broader.

In 1991, in *Renewing the Earth: An Invitation to Reflection and Action on Environment in Light of*

Catholic Social Teaching, the bishops of the United States frame the environmental crisis as a "moral challenge" that "calls us to examine how we use and share the goods of the Earth, what we pass on to future generations, and how we live in harmony with God's creation."[24] The bishops articulate specific actions, stating that they have six goals in speaking out:

- to highlight the ethical dimensions of the environmental crisis;

- to link questions of ecology and poverty, environment and development;

- to stand in solidarity with working men and women and poor and disadvantaged persons, whose lives are often impacted by ecological abuse and tradeoffs between environment and development;

- to promote a vision of a just and sustainable world community;

- to invite the Catholic community and men and women of good will to reflect more deeply on the religious dimensions of this topic; and

• to begin a broader conversation on the potential contribution of the Church to environmental questions.[25]

In *Renewing the Earth,* the U.S. bishops speak of the "goodness of all God's creation" and of humanity's "alienation from nature," stating that:

> Christian responsibility for the environment begins with appreciation of the goodness of all God's creation.... The [E]arth, the Bible reminds us, is a gift to all creatures, to all living beings – all mortal creatures that are on [E]arth.... People share the [E]arth with other creatures.... Humanity's arrogance and acquisitiveness, however, led time and again to our growing alienation from nature.[26]

On the twentieth anniversary of *This Land Is Home to Me,* the U.S. bishops of Appalachia issue *At Home in the Web of Life: A Pastoral Message on Sustainable Community in Appalachia from the Catholic Bishops in the Region* (1995), writing:

> In this letter we wish to explore the new tasks which lie before us, particularly of

creating or defending what are called "sustainable communities."

… [T]he sustainable and hopeful path sees Appalachia as a community of life, in which people and land are woven together as part of Earth's vibrant creativity, in turn revealing God's own creativity. In the vision of this path, the mountain forests are sacred cathedrals, the holy dwelling of abundant life-forms which all need each other, including us humans, with all revealing God's awesome majesty and tender embrace; empty mines are sacred wombs of Earth, opening pathways to underground rivers and to life-giving aquifers … and needing to be kept pure and clean as God's holy waters; and the people are God's co-creators, called to form sustainable communities and to develop sustainable livelihoods, all in sacred creative communion with the land and forest and water and air, indeed with all Earth's holy creatures.[27]

Sometimes people talk as if technology were the problem. We don't think that's the case, for we see the creation of technologies as part of humanity's co-creativity with the Creator. The real question, we believe, is

"Which technologies?" Does a particular technology help people or hurt them? Does it help the Earth or hurt it? The answer to this question is "appropriate technologies."[28]

Finally, at the start of the new century, in 2001, the U.S. bishops of the Northwest (with the Canadian bishop of British Columbia) issue *The Columbia River Watershed: Caring for Creation and the Common Good*, in which they articulate their "idealized ecological vision" of the Columbia Watershed community:

> In our idealized ecological vision we see the Columbia Watershed community inhabiting an environment of clean land, clear water, and pure air. In that vision the ecology is altered only by the [E]arth's natural colorations, seasonal variations, and people's responsible use of the [E]arth's goods.... They work to develop an international and intergenerational consciousness of, and respect for, the needs of the entire watershed – its people, animals, birds, fish, and plants.[29]

> People live in the world of nature, not apart from it. They need to alter that world at

times in order to provide for their needs. The means are now available to use regional resources more efficiently while doing less harm to regional ecologies. We can live in greater harmony with our surroundings if we strive to become more aware of our connection to, and responsibility for, the creation that surrounds us.[30]

We continue to hear from the world's bishops. Why are they making the environment a topic for pastoral letters, writing with such passion and conviction? Because they can see first hand what environmental devastation has done to their beautiful countries and to the lives and welfare of their people. They witness, they experience, that we humans do not exist in a vacuum but in a carefully balanced relationship with the world around us. And they are finally speaking out.

II

REMEMBERING WHAT WE ALWAYS KNEW

So, this is the "official" Catholic Church of the last three decades. But what predicates all this? Why do we need the Church to tell us that a proper respect or reverence for creation is all right, even essential? Has the Church suddenly changed its mind about nature? Or has it, along with the rest of the Western world, forgotten what it once knew?

We can certainly find themes in our Judeo/Christian tradition that support our modern disregard for nature. Mich proposes several.

One very predominant theme is our Christian fear of pantheism. In our haste to affirm that God is greater than creation, we have put God above it, outside it. We have totally separated God from nature. We have convinced ourselves that only "primitive" people believe God resides in nature. And in our minds, we have converted indigenous people's panentheist beliefs to pantheist beliefs. Pantheism is the belief that identifies God with the universe, God and creation are one. So to worship nature is to worship God. Panentheism is the belief that God resides in the world God made, and all creation resides within the God who made it since nothing can exist outside of God. Therefore, creation is reverenced as a worthy gift of a loving and generous God. It is reverenced and respected, not worshipped.

A second theme from our tradition is a disregard for this present life in favor of the next. [31] We see union in heaven as the ultimate value, making everything else secondary. Because we separated God from Earth, put God in heaven, which is up/off our planet, Earth becomes a temporary holding place, a stage. We are here but a short time. We pre-existed in the mind of God, are placed upon this Earth (this vale of tears) for a short time, then will rejoin God in heaven for all eternity when we die. Earth is not our home. Even in conversation we refer to heaven as home. When someone dies, we console the mourner by saying, "S/he has gone home to God," as if s/he were not home while here. It is no wonder we feel alienated from Earth.

This alienation leads us to one of two responses: One of these is that if Earth is not home, it doesn't really matter what we do to it. We will be saved anyway, off Earth, somewhere else in heaven. President Reagan's Secretary of the Interior, James Watt, articulated this way of thinking when he said, in response to why he was selling off timber and oil rights in national lands: It doesn't matter anyway because it will all be destroyed in rapture![32]

The other response to seeing Earth as our temporary home rests on the belief that creation was perfect until "the Fall." God made a perfect Earth, but the sin of Adam and Eve caused corruption and disease to enter the world. We have, in effect, given ourselves the ultimate "guilt trip." We have made ourselves responsible for all the chaos, turmoil, disease, sin, and even death that is in the world. In turn, we must do what we can to "fix it again." And since God promises to perfect it again in the end (God will make a new heaven and a new Earth, so we are told in Revelation), anything we can do to help is called progress.

Separating God from nature and believing this world is only a holding place has inspired *an asceticism (another theme) that basically rejects this world and sees it as a temptation that leads us away from spiritual things*, which are the greater good. (This ideology came to fruition in Jansenism, a teaching the Church condemned but one that still has a stranglehold on many of us.)

This asceticism is supported by a fourth theme, the heresy of dualistic thinking, whose destructive nature we are only now beginning to understand. Rather than seeing the world, the cosmos, as a whole, integral, interrelated, and encompassing all reality, we see it at odds with, in opposition to, itself. Listen for it. Our language is caught up in dualisms. Instead of seeing ourselves as whole persons, we see ourselves as body/soul – and at one time we abused the one to "free" other. Instead of humanity, we see white/of color, rich/poor, male/female, developed/developing. We polarize, implying that the first is better than the second, and making it all too easy to judge, dismiss, and condemn the one deemed "inferior."

A fifth theme from our tradition that helps us disregard nature is our hierarchical worldview. Everyone and everything is assigned a specific place, and woe to those who step outside it. We think in terms of ladders and pyramids rather than in terms of circles. We think exclusive rather than inclusive. We think male rather than female and male.

As ingrained as these very real and powerful Judeo/Christian cultural influences have become within us, we are not trapped. The Church has within her heritage a solid rationale for respecting and healing Earth, for understanding our role in creation. In *Renewing the Earth,* the U.S. bishops name seven Catholic moral and spiritual traditions, identifying them as "integral dimensions of ecological responsibility" (the italics are theirs):[33]

> • a *God-centered and sacramental view of the universe,* which grounds human accountability for the fate of the [E]arth;

- a consistent *respect for human life*, which extends to respect for all creation;

- a worldview affirming the ethical significance of *global interdependence and the common good*;

- an *ethics of solidarity* promoting cooperation and a just structure for sharing in the world community;

- an understanding of the *universal purpose of created things*, which requires equitable use of the [E]arth's resources;

- an *option for the poor*, which gives passion to the quest for an equitable and sustainable world;

- a conception of *authentic development*, which offers a direction for progress that respects human dignity and the limits of material growth.[34]

The bishops did not just make these up. Nothing they stated is new. They called upon the tradition and teaching of the Church in writing the pastoral.

We Catholics have a *God-centered, sacramental view of the universe*. We believe in an immanent God, an incarnational universe in which God took on our flesh. We use elements of creation in sacred worship (fire, water, oil, ashes). And our sacramental view of the universe must ground human accountability in the fate of Earth. It must demand from us our passion to co-create with God an equitable and sustainable world.

EXPLORING THE DICHOTOMIES

So, why do we have such powerful propensities that lead us to disregard nature and others that lead us to respect it? Why this conflict? Why this dichotomy, this ecotyranny versus ecoharmony, as biblical scholar Dianne Bergant calls it?[35]

There are many reasons and, like all of creation, they are interrelated. Volumes are being written, taking us back into history and developing credible explanations. Credible, even when they contradict one another.

I would like to explore another explanation. I realize it is fraught with generalizations and does not take into account all the historical nuances that, in effect, contradict the premise. But that is not my purpose. I offer it as an observation of our dichotomous behavior towards Earth.

I believe we struggle with the dichotomies, in part, because we are children, victims perhaps, of a dual heritage. As Judeo-Christians, we trace our ancestry back to two distinct traditions.

One part of our inheritance comes from the *ancient* Hebrews, not the Jews of Jesus' time but a people who would never have conceived of a natural world apart from God. These were people who saw everything as divine gift or punishment, and who would not have understood the dualisms that separated the human person into body and soul or the world into spirit and matter. The elements of their understanding of the cosmos can be seen in the early books of the Hebrew Scriptures. Anyone studying the Gospel of John knows how non-linear Hebrew thought is!

The ancient Hebrews, the early Christians, and "Western" peoples (academia notwithstanding) up to the medieval period generally took for granted that we lived in a theo-centric universe. The natural world was God's, and it was good. God, the world, and humanity were all in ordered harmony. Everything in the natural world was imbued with God's spirit. Nothing existed, nothing happened outside of God. The natural world was God's creation, and the world was the place where we would come to the knowledge of God. Thomas Aquinas tells us that, "Sacred writings are bound in two volumes, that of creation and that of holy scripture." He speaks of creation first because creation is the *primary* revelation. We came to know God in creation long before we met God in scripture.

Our inheritance, as children of the ancient Hebrew, is to think with our gut, know with our hearts, understand that the reality of the thing is far more than what we can actually observe.

The idea of the separation of matter and spirit, of body and soul, came to us not from the ancient Hebrews but from the Greeks, the other part of our heritage. The ideas of Greek philosophers already had a hold on the Jewish intellectuals of Jesus' time. They had an even greater impact on the writings of the early Church.

Plato in particular had profound influence upon Augustine, who had his own battles with the demon flesh and the world that to him represented it. Plato saw this world not as reality but as the shadow of reality (shadows on the cave wall). Reality was what you couldn't see, not what you could. Theologian Rosemary Radford Ruether tells us that, "It was from the Platonic tradition of Greek philosophy … that Western culture derived the view that evil resides in the physical body and the material world, over against the conscious mind."[36] Augustine's influence is well known and, according to Ruether, "shaped the dominant perspective of the Latin medieval world."[37]

The academic world and (with some exceptions) the hierarchy of the Church bought into Plato's understanding of reality. However, most of the common folk (the church) did not. Academia was too far removed from their daily existence to have much influence. And many of them accepted Christianity under duress, mingling it with their long-held indigenous beliefs about creation and their creator God.

Our inheritance, as children of Greek heritage, is to compartmentalize our learning, to analyze, categorize, rationalize, and hold everything up to close scrutiny, living out of our heads. Although this dualistic thinking has helped us make distinctions and formulate judgments, we have allowed it to become the lens through which we see all of reality. This unnatural polarizing of what we now know is an integrated whole has helped to create the havoc we experience in the world.

SPIRIT-VS.-MATTER DUALISM IS CHALLENGED

Although Greek thinking influenced the Church, the dualism of spirit versus matter was seen as a heresy, which raised its head again and again in the centuries following Plato. One particular outbreak in the south of thirteenth-century France inspired a young Spaniard, Dominic de Guzmán (1170-1221), to found an Order to preach against it.

To preach against the belief that made the world and all created matter evil and the invisible, spiritual realm the only good.

The teaching that all matter is evil and only the unseen spiritual is good had translated itself into a destructive lifestyle. Those who accepted the teaching were asked to renounce marriage since its purpose was to procreate more evil "matter." They were encouraged to excessive disciplining and harsh treatment of their bodies; indeed, the ultimate act of holiness was to commit suicide and free the spirit from the evil matter of the body. Fortunately, few aspired to that degree!

Dominic lived in a sacramental universe, one imbued with the presence of God. Like the Beguine mystic Mechtilde of Magdeburg (1210-c1280), Dominic saw and knew he saw "all things in God and God in all things." He preached an incarnational theology that our God took on the elements of Earth, and again declared creation itself to be good, to be holy. Dominic did not see the world as evil but as an expression of the glory of God. The founding of the Dominican Order (1216) was in direct response to the heresy that saw the created world as evil, as something to reject, to spurn. Though we have no written preachings and very few sayings of Dominic's, his followers have left an impressive imprint upon the Church and the world.

Dominican scientist Albert the Great (c1200-1280), so-called because of his renown as a scholar and teacher, picked up Dominic's theme in his own way, by doing something unheard of in academic circles. He rejected Plato's philosophy (which was the basis of all academic thought) and turned instead to Aristotle, who had basically been left on the shelf. In contrast to Plato, Aristotle taught that there is meaning, there is reality in created matter. Although he had a few problems of his own (his notion of women!), he presented a very different view of the world.

Albert was succeeded by his friend and greatest student, a Dominican named Thomas Aquinas (1225-1274). Like his teacher, Thomas looked to Aristotle rather than Plato. Although he, too, shared his teacher's misbegotten views of women (*e.g.*, calling women "misbegotten males"), Thomas makes a significant contribution to an ecotheology. While it is important not to ascribe to him our current understanding, he has much to tell us about the sacredness of creation.

Pamela Smith, SS.C.M., a systematic theologian, suggests twelve eco-themes in Thomas's great work, the *Summa Theologica*. These are:

- a faith-filled sense of the unity of the world;

- a reverence for all creatures;

- an appreciation for the simultaneous "intrinsic value" and "instrumental value" of nonhuman creatures;

- an active support of creaturely diversity;

- the extension of moral consideration to all living things;

- an exercise of providence on behalf of the universal common good;

- a healthy hierarchicalism;

- a general stance of non-aggression;

- personal moderation and the search for sustainable living;

- a commitment to Earth-healing and restoration;

- the pursuit of integrally virtuous living; and

- the study and reinterpretation of viable traditions.[38]

According to Thomas, the most marvelous thing a being can do is to be. The most wonderful thing about anything is that it is. He affirmed the visible world, in contrast to Plato, saying that everything exists in its own right and is to be taken seriously. Thomas tells us that God must be in all things, and in the most intimate manner. Creation is the overflowing of divine goodness. "God is both transcendent over creation and immanently present in each creature. Clearly no dichotomy exists between God and creatures."[39] God is present in all creation and if we want to pay tribute to the creator, we must respect the actuality, the concrete reality, the essence of all things. To do this, Thomas tells us, is more spiritual than to deny or play down the goodness of things in order to exalt some supernatural thing.

In *A Tour of the Summa*, Paul J. Glenn highlights Thomas' views about creation:

> God creates to communicate his goodness. And creatures are made to manifest or acquire perfection in the likeness of God's goodness…. Creation in the thing created, is in real relation to the Creator.[40]
>
> ....
>
> In creating, God communicates his goodness; creatures are to represent and manifest the divine goodness. And goodness, which in God is simple, in creatures is

diversified; what phase of the divine goodness one creature fails to represent may be
represented by another. The whole multi-
ple and varied universe manifests the divine
goodness more perfectly than any single
creature could do.[41]

Creation is one. Body and soul are one. There
was no dualism for Thomas.

Later in that same century, another Dominican
preacher would say, "Every creature is full of God
and is a book" about God.[42] Meister Eckhart (1260-
1327), another of Albert's students, preached an
incredible and, until now, misunderstood and little
heard message about God and creation. His words
are challenging, mind-stretching, and mystical. He
gives rich and powerful expression to our growing
understanding.

Eckhart tells us, "Creation is a revelation of God,
a home for God, a temple of God. It is a grace, an
overflow of the goodness and beauty that God is."[43]

Eckhart's awe-filled view of the visible world as
an all-encompassing revelation of God is breathtak-
ing:

All creatures want to express God in all
their works; let them all speak…. All creatures are words of God. My mouth
expresses and reveals God but the existence

50

of a stone does the same.... All creatures
may echo God in their activities.[44]

....

In fact, 'all things love God.' Loving God,
they seek God and they seek to be like God
so that it can be said that all nature seeks
God. Know that all creatures are driven and
take action by their nature for one end: to
be like God.... If God were not in all things,
nature would not accomplish or yearn for
anything ... within its very self, nature
seeks and strives for God.[45]

....

In the same love, however in which God
loves himself, he loves all creatures, not as
creatures but he loves the creatures as God.
In the same love in which God loves himself, he loves all things ... God enjoys himself. In the same enjoyment in which God
enjoys himself, he enjoys all creatures, not
as creatures, but he enjoys the creatures as
God. In the same enjoyment in which God
enjoys himself, he enjoys all things.[46]

There is no dualism here. Nor does Eckhart
speak of pantheism or nature worship. Eckhart is
simply in awe of the grace-filledness of creation. In
the passages below, he speaks of creation as the first
grace, the first manifestation of God's love and good-

ness, and of the human person as a part of this love-imbued creation.

The first kind of love which God has and which we should learn is that which completed his natural goodness to form all of creation, for in the images contained in his foreknowledge, God was pregnant with every creature from all eternity so that all creatures might enjoy with him his goodness. And among all these creatures he does not love any one more than any other. For insofar as creatures are open to receive him, to that extent God pours himself into them.[47]

....

Though we talk about human beings, we are speaking at the same time of all creatures.... God poured his being in equal measure to all creatures, to each as much as it can receive. This is a good lesson for us that we should love all creatures equally with everything which we have received from God.[48]

....

The love God bears himself contains his love for the whole world.... Every creature is on its way to the highest perfection.[49]

Creation flows out of God and back into God, and therefore we, as part of creation, must understand our relationship to it. It is all gift. Nothing is ours to own or possess. "[F]or all [God's] gifts, gifts of nature, gifts of grace, not one was made with the idea that we should regard them as our property."[50]

For Eckhart, to be unaware of pan*en*theism, says Matthew Fox, is to be ignorant, for all things are in God and God is in all things. As Fox writes on Eckhart's thought:

> For God this being in and out is no more difficult than it is for the sea that passes through the gills of a fish. God is in all things. The more he is in things, the more he is outside things: the more he is within, all the more he is without. Inside and outside are not opposed for God. We can be inside God and God can be inside us at the same time.[51]

Eckhart and Thomas both affirmed the visible world. God is present in all creation. Thomas tells us further that:

> God – every maker – leaves some sort of image of himself in what he makes, and in creatures there is a trace of the Trinity. In rational creatures there is understanding

and love. In non-rational creatures, as well, there is in that which exists a trace of the Trinity (however imperfect and faint).[52]

A trace of the Trinity! This understanding of the intimate relationship between God and creation underscores Pope John Paul's and the bishops' claim that environmental degradation is a moral issue. The loss of ecosystems and plant and animal species (both of which have a soul, according to Thomas) is no less than the destruction of a facet of the divine expression. God is diminished, and God must feel the pain of that loss.

Duquesne Theology Professor Anne Clifford, C.S.J., writes:

> From the standpoint of an ecological theology based on Aquinas' insights, the destruction of our earthly habitat suggests that discernible traces of the Trinity are lost. When species are made extinct, a unique manifestation of the goodness of God is gone forever.[53]

The ecological crisis is a cosmic crisis. It affects all parts of creation. By its very nature, no one thing can remain untouched, including humanity. The "common good," which is the sum total of all those conditions of social living that make it possible for men and women to achieve the perfection of their humanity, is at the heart of most, if not all, of the social justice documents of the Church. It serves as an arbiter to determine whether one person's particular good impinges upon the overall good of the community. Ecology is an essential part of the common good.[54] And its definition must now be broadened to embrace all of creation. Thomas and Eckhart understood this; Pope John Paul and many of the bishops now echo it.

If we have such a rich heritage of Earth spirituality in the Church and in the Dominican Order, what happened? Why do we struggle, even squirm, over expressions of this spirituality today?

Again, a little history helps.

THE PLAGUE: CHURCH AND SCIENCE PART WAYS

As mentioned earlier, most persons in the medieval world lived in a theo-centric universe, one in which God made all things and was responsible for all that happened (good or ill). Nothing happened outside of God's will. A major, catastrophic event in the fifteenth and sixteenth centuries changed not only history, but also Western culture's understanding of the role humanity plays in the world.

The bubonic plague, the Black Death, had rolled over Europe several times when rats carrying infested fleas came back from Asia with the explorers. But a recurrence of the plague this time almost decimated Europe. Somewhere between one-third and one-half of the population died horrible deaths. To the medieval mind, this disease came from nowhere. The Church didn't understand it either, and her leaders explained it only as they knew how: Since all comes from the hand of God, this terrible devastation must be divine punishment for evils committed against God.

For a growing number of scientists and mathematicians, this explanation was inadequate. Intellectuals like Kepler, Copernicus, and Galileo questioned and rejected such a view of God. Their discoveries that Earth was not the center of the universe were unappreciated by a Church whose entire moral code was based upon the assumption that it was. The Church silenced them, condemning their findings and writings. In time, the scientists began to ignore the Church, rejecting it as a source for answers to temporal matters.

The Church, in turn, began to concentrate on the Christian story, withdrawing from the world and turning its attention to salvation – off this planet – and to a theology of redemption. As science set about proving that there was no God evident in nature, the Church increasingly emphasized God as Absolute, self-sufficient, perfect, transcendent, and unaffected by the world. Church theology began to focus on saving us from this capricious world, telling us how to win the peaceful haven of heaven and leaving the study of the world to science, a most unfortunate development.[55]

The pursuit of knowledge was no longer a goal in achieving one's salvation. It now became noble for its own sake, unattached to anything else like ethics or morality.

The next two centuries (1600s-1700s) exploded in scientific thought and exploration. We call it the Age of Enlightenment, the Scientific Revolution, the Age of Reason. Thanks to men like Francis Bacon, Rene Descartes, and Isaac Newton, the scientific tone was set for the next three hundred years. Its bottom line: nature was demystified. Nature lost her soul, the animating spirit that Thomas told us she had. She became a hoarder of secrets that needed to be found out, and once found, nature could be mastered and bent to human will. Nature had become a collection of objects. The only subjects, in fact, were men.

The idea that man (the male person) was the only rational, thinking being became entrenched in our belief system. Man was the only subject in a world of objects (which included women) and man could use those objects in any way he wished. Women, like nature, had no soul. The command in Genesis that man subdue and have dominion over the Earth gave him the moral authority to do so.

Francis Bacon (1516-1626), founder of the modern scientific method, closely identified women with nature and objectified both. Theologian Elizabeth Johnson illustrates the point, writing that:

> [Bacon]… speaks of wresting new knowledge from nature's womb; of seizing her by the hair of her head and molding her into something new by technology; of penetrating her mysteries; of having the power to conquer and subdue her. He suggests that nature is a devious female similar to those women in his society who were thought to be witches. He likens the scientific method that interrogates nature to those of the juridical inquisition that examines these women, including torture with mechanical devices as a symbolic tool for wresting from nature her secrets.[56]

Rene Descartes (1596-1650) further demystified nature by giving us the image of the universe as a machine, made up only of the totality of its parts. Understand the parts, understand the whole. Isaac Newton (1642-1727) introduced us to thinking of the universe as a clock, wound up and left alone to run according to its own laws. Once we understand the laws, we understand how all things work. He also gave us the model of nature as a hierarchical pyramid: minerals on the lowest level, plant life next, lower animals next, higher animals above the lower, then children, then women, then men who capped the apex as they, alone, were the creatures made in the image and likeness of God.

Bacon, Newton and other scientists at the time were religious men, but they no longer saw God as part of creation. God was an essentially disinterested figure outside of creation. Men were at the top of the created order, and nature (as well as women, who were closely identified with nature) comprised a collection of objects to be used, abused, despoiled, and discarded as men saw fit. And because the Church had backed out, giving over the study of Earth to science, there was no guiding spirituality, no ethics, no theology to offer a different view. All that Thomas Aquinas, along with Francis of Assisi, Hildegard of Bingen, Mechtilde of Magdeburg, Meister Eckhart and others, had taught us about the God-imbued wonder of creation was ignored, lost.

The impact of this loss is felt today in the many ethical conundrums facing modern medicine and science, including DNA cloning and the genetic modification of organisms.

A New Look at an Old Faith

Church teaching today is once again reflecting the understanding we once had and lost in the last few centuries. As Catholic Christians, we do believe in the integrity of all creation. And creation refers to the whole of us, not just the part named "humanity." Creation is not only divine gift but also a manifestation of the divine goodness, an expression of the divine. We recognize that our relationship to Earth is not one of master, or even of steward, which smacks of dualism and implies that God is an "absentee landlord,"[57] living off in some distant realm.

We must look anew, for example, at our interpretation of the Genesis account of creation. The work of biblical scholar Dianne Bergant, Professor of Biblical Studies at Catholic Theological Union in Chicago, gives new insight to that ancient story. We have interpreted the creation story through the technological, Cartesian lens that views the world as a machine. This interpretation, particularly of the words to "subdue and have dominion" over nature, ignores the ancient Hebrew understanding of the truths the story is telling.[58]

Bergant tells us something we already know in our heads but have lost from our hearts: that humans and animals are made from the same stuff as Earth. Genesis tells us that; science tells us that.

Genesis also tells us that we humans are made in God's image. To the ancient Hebrew, Bergant says, this meant that humans represent, re-present, God. Humans do what God would do; they do not act for themselves. They do not represent themselves; they represent God. Even the kings of ancient Israel did not act in their own right. They represented God, ruling in God's likeness. Whenever the king's rule became absolute law in Israel, there was prophetic condemnation!

To have dominion means that humanity acts as God's representative. We exercise dominion as God does, says Bergant. And how does God act in Genesis? God acts as loving creator, providing for the needs of all, and finding everything to be very good!

Ethicist Larry Rasmussen in *Earth Community, Earth Ethics* tells us that modern Jewish exegesis of Genesis 1:28 says that "subdue and have dominion" actually means that "while all living things have some human reference and use, the proper human attitude is one of restraint, humility, and even non-interference, except in matters of necessity (such as daily bread). In fact, the modern capacity to image human beings apart from the rest of nature is largely lost to Jewish exegesis because Rabbinic Hebrew, like Biblical Hebrew, has no word for nature as a realm separate from human being or for creation as a fin-ished state."[59]

In other words, there is no human *and* nature; we are of nature. Actually, the word "nature" is rarely found in Hebrew scripture. One finds the word "cre-ation," and it is not a noun. It is a verb! It speaks the dynamic journey of an emerging universe.

The garden account of Genesis 2:5 says, "There was as yet no wild bush on the Earth nor had any wild plant yet sprung up, for God had sent no rain upon the Earth, nor was there any man to till the soil."[60] In her exegesis, Dianne Bergant points out that the word "till" in Hebrew comes from the same root as to "serve" or "preserve."

There is no fertility upon Earth because there is no one yet to till, serve, preserve it. God created Earth, but God requires humans to work alongside. Humans are to be co-creators of Earth. Earth's fertility depends upon the cooperation, co-participation of humans and God.

Bergant notes that the Hebrew word we have interpreted as "till" also means to "guard." Why guard a garden? To the ancients, a garden meant far more than our image of a plot of flowers or vegetables. It meant a sanctuary, a place where one meets God. The ancients often carved huge beings, monsters, to guard their sanctuaries. Not so much to keep people out as to remind those passing by that this marked the entrance to sacred ground. The garden, creation, was the sanctuary of God, the sacred ground where one was to meet God. The Earth is the place to meet God.

Eckhart tells us, "If the soul could have known God without the world, the world would never have been created."[61]

Adam was to till (serve and guard) Eden, Bergant says. His presence in the sanctuary reminded the rest of creation that God was present – *because being made in God's image, Adam would act as God acts*. When Adam and Eve ate of the tree of the knowledge of good and evil, they chose to become arbiters of universal truths. They committed the sin of representing themselves instead of God. And when they did, they could no longer guard the sanctuary. Others (angels by the gates) were then sent to guard Eden, and the effect of that sin disrupted Adam's relationship with Eve and with the Earth that Adam was meant to serve.

Bergant's work sheds new light on Genesis, bringing the Christian creation account more in line with those of other ancient and indigenous peoples. The Genesis story does not give us a mandate to abuse and destroy. Instead, it gives us the moral foundation to understand our interdependent role within creation. To realize that what we do to Earth we do to ourselves, as Chief Seattle so eloquently told us.

We can only be as healthy as the air we breathe, the water we drink, the soil that nourishes our food. We can only be as healthy as our fellow creatures who give us medicine, their companionship, even themselves as food, and who help us come to know God. Any diminishment of the created world is a diminishment of an aspect of the Divine expression.

Thomas Aquinas tells us that no one creature, not even the human, can adequately express God. The entire creation is needed.

More work is being done to interpret our biblical heritage in the light of the ecological crisis. A group of theologians and scripture scholars from around the globe have initiated the Earth Bible Project. They are producing a series of careful exegetical writings, whose purpose is "to identify those passages which may have contributed to the crisis and uncover those traditions which have valued Earth but been suppressed."[62]

These scholars use the following six principles as a basic approach in reading the biblical text from the perspective of Earth:

1. *The Principle of Intrinsic Worth.* The universe, Earth, and all its components have intrinsic worth and value.

2. *The Principle of Interconnectedness.* Earth is a community of interconnected living things that are mutually dependent on each other for life and survival.

3. *The Principle of Voice.* Earth is a subject capable of raising its voice in celebration and against injustice.

4. The Principle of Purpose. The universe, Earth, and all its components, are part of a dynamic cosmic design within which each piece has a place in the overall goal of that design.

5. The Principle of Mutual Custodianship. Earth is a balanced and diverse domain where responsible custodians can function as partners, rather than rulers, to sustain a balanced and diverse Earth community.

6. The Principle of Resistance. Earth and its components not only suffer from injustices at the hands of humans, but also actively resist them in the struggle for justice.[63]

These principles are used by the team to pose questions about any biblical text, utilizing the basic hermeneutic of feminist scholars: suspicion and retrieval. Using the lens of suspicion they legitimately assume that the biblical texts are anthropocentric rather than theocentric (the world whose only value is its use for humans *versus* the world as God's self-expression). Using the practice of retrieval they find features in the text that help them retrieve traditions that regard the Earth community as our kin.[64]

This is exciting work. Critics have long pointed to Christianity as a major source of the environmental crisis. It is an unfair and narrow view of a highly complex issue; no one person or group is to blame. But we share a common responsibility and a common obligation to amend the injustice.

III

DOMINICAN ROLE:
A MANDATE FOR EARTH MINISTRY

Dominicans have a special role to play in delivering the message. Dominic's calling card was "responding to the signs of the times." The needs of his day dictated a new model of religious life, one that could effectively respond to the spreading of a heresy that taught that Earth and all created matter were evil. At that time in history, men and women religious generally gathered in large monasteries and led cloistered lives, often taking a vow of stability. They were renowned for their hospitality and invited the public to come to them for respite and spiritual nourishment. But that was the problem. The "heretics" weren't coming.

Dominic knew he had to go out to them. When he announced he would build no institutions and wanted his men to walk the countryside two-by-two and mingle with the people in their homes, churches, and inns, he was severely criticized. He was told he would lose all his young men in their beautiful white habits to the first women who came along! His religious community would fail if they did not set themselves apart from the common people. How would they find time to pray and meditate?

Dominic needed mendicants and he needed teachers who knew their subject matter. He needed his followers to be preachers of the Gospel message, preachers of Truth. When Dominic announced (and received papal approbation) that his men would preach, he turned upside down the tradition that allowed only bishops that privilege. A new model! A response to the needs of the day.

The challenges of the heresy we face today are no less than the one Dominic met head on. In fact, given its scope, the challenges are considerably greater. As followers of Dominic, we are called to respond to today's needs. We are called to witness to the Truth. We are called to preach to those whose actions enslave and degrade all members of the Earth community. Like Dominic, we are to stand in solidarity with the marginated, those who have no voice. And who more so than the rivers and oceans, the depleted and toxic topsoils, mountains ravaged of their forests and minerals, the animals and plants brought to extinction through habitat loss and over-harvesting, and the human poor displaced by the insatiable consumption of the world's wealthy nations.

The ecological crisis is a human crisis. People of color and the poor most frequently suffer the worst effects of the crisis, living near landfills, toxic waste sites, city incinerators and working as farm and factory laborers exposed to toxic chemicals. Around the world, the neighborhoods and villages of the poor suffer devastation from the effects of denuded hillsides, ravaged forests, depleted soils, and polluted waters. Their "underdeveloped" countries are forced to take nuclear waste from "developed" nations and their peoples are displaced in business deals to pay off mounting national debts.

Keith Carley of the Earth Bible Project writes:

> The New Testament writer Walter Wink describes the coining of the term "ecojustice" as inspired: 'Here in a single word the connection is made between social justice and justice to life in all its forms. All justice is now ecological. All species have rights. All life is sacred."[65]

The violence we perpetrate against Earth is the same violence humans inflict upon one another. Ecojustice is not a subcategory of justice; it is a term embracing all issues of justice, because Earth is our primary reference. Without Earth, we have no life. We have no economies, no national boundaries, no way of knowing God. The paradigm or worldview that gives us license to abuse Earth is the same one that gives us license to abuse one another.

As Dominicans, we are called to understand that working to heal Earth is not a misplaced value in the light of so much human suffering. The four pillars of our life – study, preaching, common life and prayer – are foundational for responding to these signs of the time and engaging in Earth ministries.

We are called to study. As we learn what is really happening in and to our world, we are obligated to work actively and effectively to bring about equitable justice for all creation. We need to know the truth and not be derailed by the "green-washing" of many large corporations that cover up their environmental degradation with commercials (even on public television) that tug at our hearts.

We need to be wary of those who confuse the issues and create enemies (dualisms) where there should be none. The northwest logging companies, for example, clouded the issue of unsustainable clear-cutting by equating saving the spotted owl with the loss of people's jobs. People lost sight of the fact that once the trees were gone, so were the jobs! And the economic reality that there is more long-term gain in sustainable harvesting than in clear-cutting never formed part of the debate.[66]

We are called to preach. We have turned into a culture of consumers, to the detriment of the planet and all her inhabitants. Theologian Sallie McFague writes:

... [T]he planet cannot support six billion (or more) people living a Western lifestyle. As things now stand we middle-class North Americans are consuming *much* more, while others are consuming less: 20 percent of people in high-income countries account for 86 percent of private consumption, while the poorest 20 percent of the world's population consume only 1.3 percent of the pie. In Africa, the average household consumes 20 percent less than it did twenty-five years ago; two-thirds of the world's population lives on less than two dollars a day.[67]

We are called to preach the Truth that the world needs to hear about consumption gone out of control. We are called to preach about the ever-widening gap between rich and poor, about global warming and ozone depletion, about genetic manipulation and irradiation of our food supply, about the unchecked power of transnational corporations, about treatment of factory farm animals, and about species extinction and loss of habitat that will ultimately spell our own demise.

Science and technology cannot save us if we destroy the matter on which they are based. Earth is not a subcategory of the economy; the economy is based on the "gifts" of Earth.

We are called to live what we preach. A well-known and beloved Dominican story tells the point. In early efforts to thwart the doctrine that taught that Earth and all created matter were evil, the Church sent out the bishops. They arrived in the villages in full retinue, on horseback (only the rich could afford such travel), wearing fine clothes, and assisted by servants. The common folk were scandalized. In contrast to the teachers of the heresy, who lived poorly and simply among the people, these bishops were not credible. Why should the people listen to them?

Dominic understood the need for credible witness. He and his men traveled on foot, wearing simple robes, begging for food and lodging. When offered hospitality, they preached in the inns, in village markets, in people's homes. We, too, must be credible witnesses to the Truths we preach. We must consume less. We must utilize appropriate and sustainable means for lighting and heating our buildings. We must make healthy choices about the food we eat, the clothes we wear, the places we shop. Our preaching is only as credible as the choices we make to live more simply, more sustainably with Earth.

"Eco" comes from the Greek word for "oikos," which means household. Earth is the household. It is the only context for all we do and all that we are as humans. To live sustainably means to live as responsible inhabitants of the entire community that makes up the household of Earth. Sallie McFague put it this way. We must "abide by three main rules: take only your share, clean up after yourselves, and keep the house in good repair for future occupants."[68]

We are called to prayer. The call to study, to preach Truth, to live as credible witnesses are not just the domain of Dominicans. All of us are called to these, as we are all called to prayer (the fourth pillar). How often have we heard that prayer changes things? We say we believe it. Yet we often act as though we don't. Some of us have experienced personal conversion through prayer. Some of us have witnessed situations change for the better after our prayer. But for the most part, prayer has been relegated to the realm of religion, to the purview of the Church.

Now, science may be lending "proof" that prayer is "more" than a religious notion, that it is an actual and effective tool for change. Quantum physics teaches us that everything, without exception, is part of the whole, and that the whole is greater than the sum of its parts. Total autonomy, separateness, does not exist anywhere in this universe. What happens in any one part of the universe, on any level, profoundly affects every other part of the universe.

Diarmuid O'Murchu writes,

> In quantum mechanics, two subatomic particles can interact locally and then move

very far apart. But the rules of quantum physics are such that even if the particles end up on opposite sides of the universe, they must be treated as an indivisible whole. This was ably demonstrated in Aspect's experiment of 1982, when two identical photons were emitted by a calcium atom in opposite directions. It was noted that if certain influences were brought to bear on one of the photons, then the second photon is also affected, although the latter may be on the other side of the moon.[69]

Quantum physics has turned our mechanistic, Newtonian world literally upside down. Quantum physics is teaching us a whole new reality. Actually, it is reaffirming an old one: Our faith has always taught us that prayer changes things. Perhaps science is now proving that.

Utilizing quantum physics, philosopher Danah Zohar presents a compelling case for the power of prayer. She speaks of the nature of thought and creativity in our quantum universe and proposes that consciousness can be explained as a quantum process.

[O]nce we have seen that the physics of human consciousness emerges from quantum processes within the brain and that in consequence human consciousness and the whole world of its creation shares a physics with everything else in this universe – with the human body, with all other living things and creatures, with the basic physics of matter and relationship, and with the coherent ground state of the quantum vacuum itself – it becomes impossible to imagine a single aspect of our lives that is not drawn into one coherent whole.[70]

Because of the intimate connection between every particle in the universe, every action has an effect on the whole. Our every thought (good or ill) has a physical effect not only on ourselves but also on humanity's shared consciousness. Zohar writes:

This is the reality of Saint Paul's warning that the sin is in the thought…. The same applies to filling the mind with any sort of suggestion…. Even if we don't act on the temptations they raise, the temptations themselves affect the general health of our individual and shared consciousness.[71]

She further states, "There is no end to the chain of influence that follows from my decision. I am responsible for the world because I help to make the world."[72]   This idea echoes what Erich Heller expressed when he said, "Be careful how you interpret the world; it *is* like that."[73]

A frightening thought. Yet also an exhilarating one. It affirms the power of our being affected by the violence and hopelessness of the world, even if we do not experience it first hand. And it similarly means that all the hope-filled efforts of many good people also affect us, and that our consciousness, our thoughts, our prayer impact the whole. This must give us consummate hope that our work and the choices we make for the common good of all creation are helping to bring about the very changes we seek.

Quantum physics gives us the scientific explanation for a phenomenon that people of faith have long held as true: Prayer can change the world.

CONCLUSION

In *The Body of God*, Sallie McFague reminds us that any image we have of God can only be a metaphor. Yet we have turned our image of God into a *definition*, a definition based on the rationalistic, mechanistic worldview given to us during the Enlightenment. It is time, says McFague, to reclaim the classic organic model of God that sees the universe as God's body, the expression of a God whose love is so great it spills over in extravagant and lavish creativity. That model is coming to us again not from the churches (unfortunately), but from science.

As science and religion begin to repair their long-standing breach through earnest and open dialogue (and these meetings are happening all over the world), we can hope that they model what the universe teaches us – interdependence and interrelatedness. The Catholic Church has always excelled in telling the story of our faith. Science now gives us more of the facts than we ever knew previously in history. It is time that both share the common story in a way that is relevant to this century and mobilizes us for appropriate action.

Quantum physics changes our understanding of Earth and the universe. We move away from seeing creation as the sum total of a set of building blocks to comprehending creation as a web of relationships. Science, in other words, is revealing that we can no longer look upon Earth as an object; our relationship to her must be as subject-to-subject. Our Catholic tradition supports and expands this insight, revealing that all subjects in God's creation, animate and inanimate, are imbued with the love and presence of God.

What *is* God's call in the world?

Seeing through the lens of our twentieth-century worldview, we religious have understood God's call as a challenge for us to respond to the dire needs of poor and oppressed people, here in our own nation and around our world. We responded to that call with our hearts, our lives, and our resources.

But now we are putting on a new lens, a millennial lens. And we see that God's call in the world is nothing less than God speaking in and through each and every subject in our world. Every living person, every blade of grass, every whiff of wind and burst of color, every wetland and river, every cornfield, puddle, pebble, and oak. Every croak, caw, bellow, chirp, and sob. We all accompany one another on this one cosmic journey. We are all related. We are all part of the whole. God's call in the world challenges us to take off the blinders that focused our attention only on humanity. It is time for us to act not only in the name of humanity, but in the name of the entire community of Earth.

NOTES

[1] Marvin L. Krier Mich, CATHOLIC SOCIAL TEACHING AND MOVEMENTS (Mystic, Conn.: Twenty-Third Publications, 1998), p. 386.

[2] Deborah Blake, "Toward a Sustainable Ethic: Virtue and the Environment," AND GOD SAW THAT IT WAS GOOD: CATHOLIC THEOLOGY AND THE ENVIRONMENT, edited by Drew Christiansen, S.J. and Walter Grazer (Washington, D.C.: United States Catholic Conference, 1996), p. 199.

[3] Mich, CATHOLIC SOCIAL TEACHING, p. 386.

[4] Mich, CATHOLIC SOCIAL TEACHING, p. 386.

[5] Sean McDonagh, TO CARE FOR THE EARTH: A CALL TO A NEW THEOLOGY (Santa Fe: Bear & Company, 1987), p. 5.

[6] Mich, CATHOLIC SOCIAL TEACHING, p. 388.

[7] Drew Christiansen, S.J., "Ecology and the Common Good: Catholic Social Teaching and Environmental Responsibility," AND GOD SAW THAT IT WAS GOOD: CATHOLIC THEOLOGY AND THE ENVIRONMENT, ed. by Drew Christiansen, S.J. and Walter Grazer (Washington, D.C.: United States Catholic Conference, 1996) p. 190.

[8] United States Catholic Conference, *Renewing the Earth: An Invitation to Reflection and Action on Environment in Light of Catholic Social Teaching* (Washington, D.C.: USCC, 1996), p. 10.

[9] Christine Firer Hinze, "Catholic Social Teaching and Ecological Ethics," AND GOD SAW THAT IT WAS GOOD, pp. 178-179.

[10] John Paul II, *The Ecological Crisis: A Common Responsibility – Peace with God the Creator, Peace with All Creation* (Vatican City: January 1, 1990), par. 16.

[11] *Ibid.*, par. 13.

[12] *Ibid.*, par. 1.

[13] *Ibid.*, par. 13.

[14] *Ibid.*, par. 15.

[15] *Ibid.*, par. 16.

[16] *Ibid.*, par. 16.

[17] Mich, CATHOLIC SOCIAL TEACHING, p. 390.

[18] John Paul, *The Ecological Crisis*, par. 16.

[19] Mich, CATHOLIC SOCIAL TEACHING, p. 393.

[20] Catholic Bishops of Appalachia, *This Land Is Home to Me: A Pastoral Letter on Powerlessness in Appalachia* (Webster Springs, West Virginia: 1975), p. 7.

[21] *Ibid.*, p. 11.

[22] Catholic Bishops of the Midwest, *Strangers and Guests: Toward Community in the Heartland* (1980), p. 2, par. 7.

[23] The texts of the pastorals of the bishops outside the United States are found in the appendix of AND GOD SAW THAT IT WAS GOOD: CATHOLIC THEOLOGY AND THE ENVIRONMENT.

[24] United States Catholic Conference, *Renewing the Earth: An Invitation to Reflection and Action on Environment in Light of Catholic Social Teaching* (Washington, D.C.: 1991), Section I, par. 1.

[25] *Ibid.*, Section I, par. 5.

[26] *Ibid.*, Section II, par. 1-4.

[27] Catholic Bishops of Appalachia, *At Home in the Web of Life: A Pastoral Message on Sustainable Community in*

Appalachia from the Catholic Bishops in the Region (Webster Springs, West Virginia: 1995), p. 5.

[28] *Ibid.*, p. 47.

[29] Catholic Bishops of the Northwest, *The Columbia River Watershed: Caring for Creation and the Common Good* (Helena, Montana: Insty Prints/Century-Printers: 2001), p.11.

[30] *Ibid.*, p. 17.

[31] Miriam Therese MacGillis, O.P. presented the ideas elaborated here at a conference titled *Recovering a Sense of the Whole: Coming Home to the Community of Life* at Siena Spirituality Center in Water Mill, New York (March 29-31, 1996).

[32] Al Gore, EARTH IN THE BALANCE: ECOLOGY AND THE HUMAN SPIRIT, (New York: Plume, 1993), p. 263.

[33] Mich, CATHOLIC SOCIAL TEACHING AND MOVEMENTS, p. 402.

[34] United States Catholic Conference, *Renewing the Earth,* pp. 5-6.

[35] Dianne Bergant, "The Wisdom of Solomon," READINGS FROM THE PERSPECTIVE OF EARTH, ed. by Norman C. Habel (Sheffield, England: Sheffield Academic Press, 2000), p. 141.

[36] Rosemary Radford Ruether, GAIA & GOD: AN ECOFEMINIST THEOLOGY OF EARTH HEALING (San Francisco: Harper, 1992), p. 122.

[37] *Ibid.*, p. 186.

[38] Mich, CATHOLIC SOCIAL TEACHING, p. 405.

[39] Anne M. Clifford, "Foundations for a Catholic Ecological Theology and the Environment," AND GOD SAW THAT IT WAS GOOD, p. 39.

[40] Paul J. Glenn, A TOUR OF THE SUMMA (St. Louis: B. Herder Book, Co., 1960), p. 40.

[41] *Ibid.*, p. 42.

[42] Raymond Blakney, trans., MEISTER ECKHART (New York: Harper & Row, 1941), p. 222.

[43] Matthew Fox, BREAKTHROUGH: MEISTER ECKHART'S CREATION SPIRITUALITY IN NEW TRANSLATION (New York: Image Books, 1980), p. 55.

[44] *Ibid.*, p. 58.

[45] *Ibid.*, p. 63.

[46] *Ibid.,* p. 76.

[47] *Ibid.*, p. 91.

[48] *Ibid.*, p. 92.

[49] Blakney, MEISTER ECKHART, p. 225.

[50] *Ibid.*, p. 38.

[51] Fox, BREAKTHROUGH, p. 73.

[52] Glenn, A TOUR OF THE SUMMA, p. 41.

[53] Clifford, "Foundations," AND GOD SAW THAT IT WAS GOOD, p. 39.

[54] Christiansen, "Ecology and the Common Good," AND GOD SAW THAT IT WAS GOOD, p. 185.

[55] The divergent roads of science and religion lasted centuries. Only now are we witnessing the beginnings of a dialogue between the two, perhaps the beginning of the end of the schism and distrust.

[56] Elizabeth A. Johnson, WOMEN, EARTH, AND CREATOR SPIRIT (New Jersey: Paulist Press, 1993), p.15.

[57] Diarmuid O'Murchu, POVERTY, CELIBACY, AND OBEDIENCE: A RADICAL OPTION FOR LIFE (New York: Crossroad, 1999), p. 66.

[58] Dianne Bergant, THE EARTH IS THE LORD'S, magnetic tape (Canfield, Ohio: Alba House, 1992).

[59] Larry Rasmussen, EARTH COMMUNITY, EARTH ETHICS (New York: Orbis Books, 1996), p. 231.

[60] The New Jerusalem Bible.

[61] Blakney, MEISTER ECKHART, p. 161.

[62] Norman C. Habel, ed., READINGS FROM THE PERSPECTIVE OF EARTH (Sheffield, England: Sheffield Academic Press, 2000), p. 7.

[63] *Ibid.*, p. 24.

[64] *Ibid.*, p. 39.

[65] Keith Carley, "Psalm 8: An Apology for Domination," READINGS FROM THE PERSPECTIVE OF EARTH, ed. by Norman C. Habel (Sheffield, England: Sheffield Academic Press, 2000), p.112.

[66] A number of economists like Herman Daly, who coauthored FOR THE COMMON GOOD with theologian John Cobb, Jr., and Paul Hawken, author of THE ECOLOGY OF COMMERCE, suggest viable alternatives.

[67] Sally McFague, LIFE ABUNDANT: RETHINKING ECOLOGY AND ECONOMY FOR A PLANET IN PERIL (Minneapolis: Fortress Press, 2001), p. 88.

[68] *Ibid.*, p. 122.

[69] Diarmuid O'Murchu, QUANTUM THEOLOGY: SPIRITUAL IMPLICATIONS OF THE NEW PHYSICS (New York: Crossroad Publishing, 1999), p. 57.

[70] Danah Zohar, THE QUANTUM SELF: HUMAN NATURE AND CONSCIOUSNESS DEFINED BY THE NEW PHYSICS (New York: Quill/William Morrow, 1990), p. 236.

[71] *Ibid.*, p. 196.

[72] *Ibid.*, p.198.

[73] McFague, LIFE ABUNDANT, p. 181.

RECOMMENDED RESOURCES

Below is a list of books and videos that were influential in Sharon Zayac's thinking and that currently inspire her:

Capra, Fritjof. THE TAO OF PHYSICS. Boston: Shambhala, 1991.

Edwards, Denis. THE GOD OF EVOLUTION: A TRINITARIAN THEOLOGY. New York: Paulist Press, 1999.

Fox, Matthew. ORIGINAL BLESSING. Santa Fe: Bear & Co., 1983.

Fox, Matthew. BREAKTHROUGH: MEISTER ECKHART'S CREATION SPIRITUALITY IN NEW TRANSLATION. New York: Image Books, 1980.

Gebara, Ivone. LONGING FOR RUNNING WATER: ECOFEMINISM AND LIBERATION. Trans. David Molineaux . Minneapolis: Fortress Press, 1999.

Haught, John. GOD AFTER DARWIN: A THEOLOGY OF
EVOLUTION. Boulder: Westview, 2000.

McFague, Sallie. THE BODY OF GOD: AN ECOLOGICAL
THEOLOGY. Minneapolis: Fortress Press, 1993.

O'Murchu, Diarmuid. QUANTUM THEOLOGY:
SPIRITUAL IMPLICATIONS OF THE NEW THEOLOGY. New
York: Crossroads, 1997.

Rasmussen, Larry. EARTH COMMUNITY EARTH ETHICS.
New York: Orbis, 1996.

Video Series: Swimme, Brian. *Canticle to the
Cosmos*. Livermore, California: Center for the
Story of the Universe, 1990.

POSTSCRIPT: ABOUT THIS SERIES

Beginning in the thirteenth century, a new form of theology emerged in which women, "for the first time in Christianity, took on an important, perhaps even preponderant role," writes Bernard McGinn in the introduction to MEISTER ECKHART AND THE BEGUINE MYSTICS.[1]

"Vernacular" theology differed both in content and audience from the academic concerns of scholastic theology and the biblical commentary of monastic theology. Written not in Latin but in the spoken language of medieval people, vernacular theology "implied a different and wider audience than that addressed by traditional monastic and scholastic theology."[2]

Among those who contributed significantly to the body of vernacular theology were the Beguines, women in Europe who took up a nontraditional form of independent and apostolic religious life beginning in the twelfth century.

Written by nontraditional women in a nontraditional language, the vernacular teachings also came in nontraditional forms.

According to McGinn, "Much of it was expressed in sermonic form, though of many kinds. A wide variety of treatises and 'little books' were employed, as well as hagiography and letters. Poetry was also of significance."[3]

We draw upon this rich thirteenth-century tradition in publishing this series of "little books," written by Dominican women in a vernacular created out of the soil of their experience of living into new ways of being human, at the dawn of the twenty-first century. These new ways of being are impelled by an inchoate awareness of our place in the universe and by the shocking awareness of an imperiled Earth.

The first awareness: In the last quarter of the twentieth century, insights gleaned from new scientific understandings about the nature and origin of our universe have been applied by a host of writers in a variety of fields, including theology, to revisit assumptions derived from a more than 300-year-old understanding of the universe as a static, mechanistic and hierarchically ordered object. The writings reflect the profound psychic shift we have undergone in seeing, for the first time in human history, our home planet from outer space; in learning about the deep interconnectedness of all life; in reawakening, through scientific inquiry, to the ancient revelation of "Oneness" that all our spiritual traditions teach; and in understanding our place in the universe as a self-aware, conscious species inhabiting a "privileged" planet, where life has emerged through an epic thirteen-billion-year journey that is still unfolding in form and consciousness.

The second: With the public stir created by the publication of Rachel Carson's SILENT SPRING in 1962, as Sharon Zayac, O.P. points out in EARTH SPIRITUALITY: IN THE CATHOLIC AND DOMINICAN TRADITIONS[4], the modern environmental movement began. Since then, innumerable reports, studies, and books have been written, documenting the extraordinary assault on Earth's life systems undertaken by humans during the past 100 years. Life on Earth has not been this threatened since 65 million years ago when, as scientists now believe, a six-mile-wide asteroid plunged into the ocean off the Yucatan Peninsula. Dinosaurs were among the many species that went extinct in the ensuing nuclear darkness; it took some ten to fifteen million years for Earth to recover from the disaster.[5]

In response to these signs of the times, many groups and individuals around the globe have begun to act, including women religious. Among congregations of Catholic Sisters, many are approaching their own "motherlands" differently: conserving land, creating wildlife habitat, letting fields lie fallow, converting to organic growing, exploring alternative energy usage. A number of women religious around the world have established ecological centers dedicated to teaching Earth literacy, modeling ways of living lightly on the land, understanding systemic connections of oppression among all forms of domination, exploring Earth spirituality, cultivating diversity, and nurturing sustainable relationships among all creation.

Of the three-dozen or so ecological centers and initiatives that have been created by women religious in the United States, more than a third were founded or co-founded by Dominican sisters (see list, p. 97). Best known among these is Genesis Farm, founded in 1980 by Caldwell Dominican Miriam Therese MacGillis, O.P., whose inspiring example helped give birth to so many of the other centers.

The authors of this series are Dominican women who, like Miriam and women in other religious communities, are living into and sharing new ways of being human on Earth. Actually, these are ways that indigenous peoples have long known and lived and that all humans are now being called to learn, drawing on their own spiritual traditions, if our species is to survive.

For many Catholics, the unfolding "Universe Story" and "new" Earth spirituality are wonder-filled invitations to go deeper into the mysteries of their faith; to plumb its incarnational and sacramental essence. Teilhard de Chardin grasped the awesomeness of it all when he wrote:

The sacramental Species are formed by the totality of the world, and the duration of the creation is the time needed for its consecration.[6]

Seven hundred years earlier, Beguine mystic Mechtild of Magdeburg (1210-c1280) had intuited this Oneness, writing:

> The day of my spiritual awakening
>   was the day I saw
>   and knew I saw
>   all things in God
>   and God
>   in all things.[7]

More practical than mystical, Sor Juana Inés de la Cruz (1648 -1695) – the Mexican nun, scientist, poet, musician, and scholar whose memory is honored by the Sor Juana Press – dedicated herself to "reading" the natural world through observation on the several occasions when she was forbidden to read books. Believing that knowledge of the arts and sciences was the path to knowledge of God, Sor Juana wrote:

> It seem[s] to me debilitating for a Catholic not to know everything in this life of the Divine Mysteries that can be learned through natural means...[8]

It is our hope that these "little books" will stimulate an engaging *conversatio* ("living with a familiarity that includes but is not limited to verbal discussion"[9]) among women religious and others about both the issues each author presents and the spiritual journey she shares. In particular, we hope that each "little book" will stimulate deep *conversatio* around questions of faith, spirituality, and Divine consciousness.

- Editors

[1] MEISTER ECKHART AND THE BEGUINE MYSTICS, ed. by Bernard McGinn (New York: Continuum, 1994), p. 6.

[2] *Ibid.*, p. 8.

[3] *Ibid.*, p. 9.

[4] Sharon Zayac, O.P., EARTH SPIRITUALITY: IN THE CATHOLIC AND DOMINICAN TRADITIONS, Dominican Women on Earth, ed. by Elise D. García and Carol Coston, O.P. (San Antonio, Texas: Sor Juana Press, 2003), p. 18.

[5] See Tim Flannery, THE ETERNAL FRONTIER: AN ECOLOGICAL HISTORY OF NORTH AMERICA AND ITS PEOPLES (New York: Grove Press, 2001), pp. 9-24.

[6] Pierre Teilhard de Chardin, THE DIVINE MILIEU (New York: Harper & Row, Publishers, 1968), p. 126.

[7] Sue Woodruff, MEDITATIONS WITH MECHTILD OF MAGDEBURG (Santa Fe, New Mexico: Bear & Company, Inc., 1982), p. 42.

[8] Sor Juana Inés de la Cruz, "Response to the Most Illustrious Poetess Sor Filotea de la Cruz," A WOMAN OF GENIUS: THE INTELLECTUAL AUTOBIOGRAPHY OF SOR JUANA INÉS DE LA CRUZ, trans. by Margaret Sayers Peden (Salisbury, Conn.: Lime Rock Press, Inc., 1982), p. 32.

[9] See McGuinn, MEISTER ECKHART, p. 8, where he refers to "Meister Eckhart's 'conversation' with the Beguines (understood in the Latin sense of *conversatio*, that is, living with a

familiarity that includes but is not limited to verbal discussion)" as providing "a particularly instructive example" of ways in which "medieval mystical texts challenge stereotypes about men and women...."

ECOLOGY/ECOSPIRITUALITY CENTERS

Established by Women Religious in the United States
(Known to editors as of May 2003)

ALLIUM
LaGrange Park, Illinois
Sisters of St. Joseph of LaGrange

THE BRIDGE BETWEEN
Denmark, Wisconsin
Sinsinawa Dominican Sisters

CEDAR HILL ENRICHMENT CENTER
Gainsville, Georgia
Adrian Dominican Sisters

CENTER FOR EARTH SPIRITUALITY AND RURAL MINISTRY
Mankato, Minnesota
School Sisters of Notre Dame

CHURCHES' CENTER FOR LAND AND PEOPLE
Sinsinawa, Wisconsin
Sinsinawa Dominican Sisters

CLARE'S WELL
Annandale, Minnesota
Franciscan Sisters of Little Falls

CROWN POINT ECOLOGY LEARNING CENTER
Bath, Ohio
Sisters of St. Dominic of Akron

CRYSTAL SPRING
Plainville, Massachusetts
Kentucky Dominican Sisters

DOMINICAN REFLECTION CENTER
Edmonds, Washington
Dominican Sisters of Edmonds

EARTHEART
La Casa de María Retreat Center
Santa Barbara, California
La Casa de María/Immaculate Heart Community
Sisters of St. Joseph, Los Angeles Province
Religious of Sacred Heart of Mary, Western America
Province

EARTHLINKS
Denver, Colorado
Loretto Community
Dominican Sisters of Hope

EVERGREEN
Villa Maria, Pennsylvania
Sisters of Humility of Mary at Villa Maria

FRANCISCAN EARTH LITERACY CENTER
Tiffin, Ohio
Tiffin Franciscans

FRANKLIN FARM
Manchester, New Hampshire
Sisters of Holy Cross

GENESIS FARM
Blairstown, New Jersey
Caldwell Dominican Sisters

GRAILVILLE
Loveland, Ohio
Grailville Community

GREEN MOUNTAIN MONASTERY
N. Chittenden, Vermont
Passionist Sisters of the Earth Community

HEARTLAND FARM AND SPIRITUALITY CENTER
Pawnee Rock, Kansas
Great Bend Dominican Sisters

JUBILEE FARM
New Berlin, Illinois
Springfield Dominican Sisters

MERCY ECOLOGY INSTITUTE
Madison, Connecticut
Sisters of Mercy

MICHAELA FARM
Oldenburg, Indiana
Sisters of St. Francis of Oldenburg

NAZARETH FARM AND CENTER FOR ENVIRONMENTAL
SPIRITUALITY
Kalamazoo, Michigan
Sisters of St. Joseph of Nazareth

PRAIRIE WOODS FRANCISCAN SPIRITUALITY CENTER
Hiawatha, Iowa
Franciscan Sisters of Perpetual Adoration

RED HILL FARM
Acton, Pennsylvania
Sisters of St. Francis of Philadelphia

SANTUARIO SISTERFARM
Welfare, Texas
Adrian Dominican Sisters

SHEPHERD'S CORNER
Blacklick, Ohio
Columbus Dominican Sisters

SIENA SPIRITUALITY CENTER
Water Mill, New York
Amityville Dominicans

SISTERS HILL FARM
Bronx, New York
Sisters of Charity New York

SOPHIA GARDEN
Amityville, New York
Amityville Dominican Sisters

SPRINGBANK RETREAT CENTER
Kingstree, South Carolina
Adrian Dominican Sisters
Sisters of St. Francis of Oldenburg

ST. CATHARINE FARM/DOMINICAN EARTH CENTER
St. Catharine, Kentucky
Dominicans of St. Catharine, Kentucky

WATERSPIRIT
Elberon, New Jersey
Sisters of St. Joseph of Peace

WHITE VIOLET CENTER FOR ECO-JUSTICE
Saint Mary-of-the-Woods, Indiana
Sisters of Providence of Saint Mary-of-the-Woods

THE WOODLANDS
Osseo, Wisconsin
Sisters of St. Francis of Assisi

Note: In addition to establishing ecology and/or ecospirituality centers, women religious in the United States and in a number of countries around the world are engaged in an array of activities aimed at conserving land, promoting sustainable practices, restoring natural habitats, and modeling new ways of living lightly on Earth. Descriptions of a number of these efforts can be found on the website of the National Catholic Rural Life Conference (see www.ncrlc.com) and in the annotated directory of members of Sisters of Earth, a network of women dedicated to healing Earth's community of life, founded in 1994 by a group of concerned women religious (see www.sistersofearth.org). As more centers are identified we will include them in ensuing publications.

Among the many outstanding examples of ecological efforts underway is the "Ecovillage" project completed in April 2003 by the Sisters, Servants of the Immaculate Heart of Mary (IHMs) of Monroe, Michigan. The IHMs invested $56 million in a massive effort to renovate their 376,000-square-foot motherhouse in an environmentally conscious way, developing, among other things, geothermal wells for heating and cooling and a graywater system for reusing water that will cut consumption by thirty-five percent (see www.ihmsisters.org).

Several communities have established congregation-wide ecology committees, such as the Loretto

Community's Earth Network Coordinating Committee, to share information, plan ecology projects, sponsor educational events, and motivate the membership to a deeper ecological sensitivity. Some congregations focus on raising ecological consciousness and practices at their motherhouses. For example, the Adrian Dominicans' Earth Stewardship Promoters sponsors educational seminars and has set up an ecology resource room, coordinated the establishment of a wetlands and a Cosmic Walk on campus grounds, and advocated successfully the switch to post-consumer recycled paper for office supplies.

Others are involved in inter-congregational efforts. In 1998, twelve congregations of women religious, along with other Catholic institutions that own land in the Hudson River bio-region of New York, set up ROAR (Religious Organizations Along the River) to "support one another in using our lands with an attitude of respect for beauty and integrity of Earth" and to "address the interrelated issues of poverty, justice and ecology in this bio-region."